# WESTERLY WINDS

## ON MARS

# *WESTERLY WINDS*
## *ON MARS*

**A POETRY AND PHOTOGRAPHY COLLECTION**

**Mr Peroxide**

First paperback edition published on the 8Th of February 2021

Second paperback edition published on the 16th of February 2021

Second edition included changes to font size, and formatting issues.

Photography by Mr Peroxide

Poems by Mr Peroxide

Cover design by Mr Peroxide

ISBN 9798597535746 (paperback)

www.mrperoxidephotography.com

For those who love obscurity

for those who look at the stars and wish for more

for those who enjoy the comfort in photography and poetry

may it all sit nicely in your hand

at home

on the train

at work

or

in bed

*mr peroxide*

# CONTENTS

# CONTENTS

# *WESTERLY WINDS ON MARS*

## SADNESS GIVEN UNAPOLOGETICALLY

Slow beat, beating heart
To scribbled lead on torn pages
Underachiever
Crush me, crushing down to my knees
Cracks the body that contains it
Sadness. Spiralling inadequacy,
Seeping back through
Each salty drop.

Finding it myself,
I bleed through to you.
I scream this is my sadness, never good enough.
Can you hear me? This is my sadness.
Given unapologetically.

Touching the face of god,
Smoke pot.

## WESTERLY WINDS ON MARS

Lockdown and Locked in.
Sipping celestially infused tea,
Watching whipping westerly winds
Ripping through,
Terraformed lands,
Headphones in
70's bands.

Winds swiping up through broken floorboards of our
South coast cottage abode in Northern Mars.
Sadness rush
Hand in hand
Meeting in bitter friendship.
Admiring not one, not two
But thousands of other lonely stars.

## SEEKING HOPE ON BARREN BEECHES

Treacherous oceans washed through our home,
Currents crashing through memories
Forming perfect maelstrom
Only taking.

I lie
Reasoning that the moon and the stars
Aligned to engulf me.
How wrong I was to find out
Rouge waves produced by your
Unsettled mind did capsize.

The oceans that once cradled our children
Now toxic, filled with hatred
Slowly calming to stagnant resolve
No space for me, no reconciliation

Washed up by a tidal bore
Defeated, seeking hope on barren beeches
No life, searching for something new

*Mr Peroxide*

*Sitting in the palm of your hand*

*You look at my body*

*Make a fist and crush it*

SANDHANDS

You stabbed into my bare chest and
Forcibly opened up my punctured lungs
To let the fully
Oxygenated lush forest of my love
Pour out
Into your hands

You let it fall through the cracks
Like sand

I FELT SORRY FOR ME

Sulking deeply, shadowy abandon
In the nightclub smoking area
Resisting silent tears
Slowly building behind each pale blue pupil.
Unnoticed at first, until
A cigarette was offered,
Then lit by a stranger
Pacifying my quivering
Salt-soaked bottom lip.
Unaware of the fact I seldom smoke.
They felt sorry for me.

I felt sorry for me.

## POENA CULLEI

I had no regrets
I waved
Goodbye father
Committed a crime of
Mental parricide
Sewn in for death
My last bubbles of breath
Going travelling up
Feet firmly embedded
Snake squished beside me
My own body the anchor
For once, I was clearheaded
Only now
I am free

DRUNK

Acidic rushes
Wine flowing
Running
Racing
To vomit out
The last part of you.

Attempted focus
Greeted with blurry waters
With only brief moments of still…
Before I vomited.
The bowl to fill.

Counting now five times over
Never enough to escape
The red wine slurry
I had hit the sin-soaked finish line

I wake to wine-stained lips,
And do it all over again.

## TO FALSE EMBRACE

Two bodies close
Naked,
Gently guided, slithered through
Doorway opening.

A garden discovered.
Finding only Gods,
Evil twin.
Escape to no success,
To false embrace.

## HEMLOCK MARTINI

If hell froze its wild flame
You would still be a blaze
Coal heart hell man
White burn
I knew you would come
The vipers tongue.

Mighty prophet
You awaken at night
Under his menacing eye
Yours to contend with mine
Pocket watch
Tik tok
Goes the clock
Sipping the nightclubs Hemlock.

## ALONE AGAIN NATURALLY

Friendship or love
Whatever it is
I'm tired of begging for it
Here I am again,
Alone again naturally

## THOSE FOUR WALLS

Damn it you've done it again

Twice already in the new year

These four fresh white walls

That makes my bedroom

Judging me silently

Suffocating my violently

Taking in each frail moment

Spinning to see each wall looking

The same

Day to day

It just took me 4 months to paint

Over the black

But I'll spend a year slowly staining

These virgin whites

Through greys

To darker shades

Until I'm sat again

Peacefully in black

Where I most feel at home

But most alone.

## HUMMINGBIRD

Close those curtains before sunrise
Shield me
And my dreams, deep
Swirling sweet in fetal sleep.

I couldn't bare seeing out
Nor the sun seeing in
On worn white sheets
To paler skin.

The Sun Guard on 6 am duty
Mother nature's wakeup call
Soft and gentle sun rise
Through the forest trees
Its rays now much harsher
When it got down to business with me.

I drew them back
Those curtains
To be greeted sweetly
By the Hummingbird
She was only singing for me.

## MIGRAINE

Bitter migraine

I endure you knocking again

Lurking and forcing your way

To get inside of my brain

Violently stabbing each sinew for entry

You continue to abuse me

Even unwelcome I could see you

The thief, to steal my day


I do not even let my friends

Touch me like you do

So intimately swirling around my brain

To curl up slowly

Pulsing pain

In covered darkened room

Curtains drawn, eyes tight shut

Maybe if I clawed my eyes out and

Ate them

It would force you away

Make you disappear

I beg you

Get out of my brain

Two small tablets from my bedside table

My western medicine lifeboats

Come to save me in water with two mighty gulps


Gulp

Gulp


Your petty swirls, your white enigmas

My impaired vision does not fool me

Despise those dizzy eyes.

You almighty migraine

Get out of my brain.

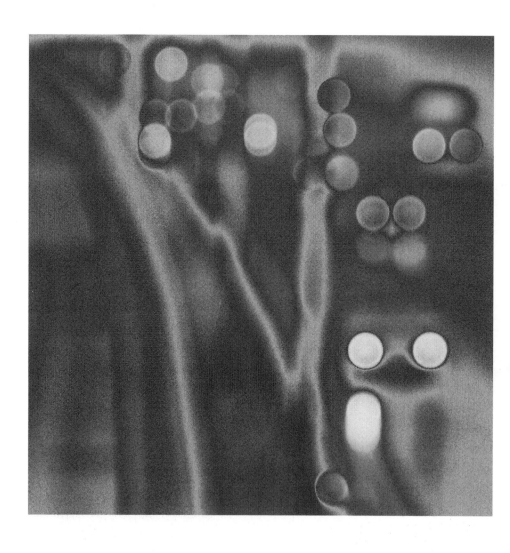

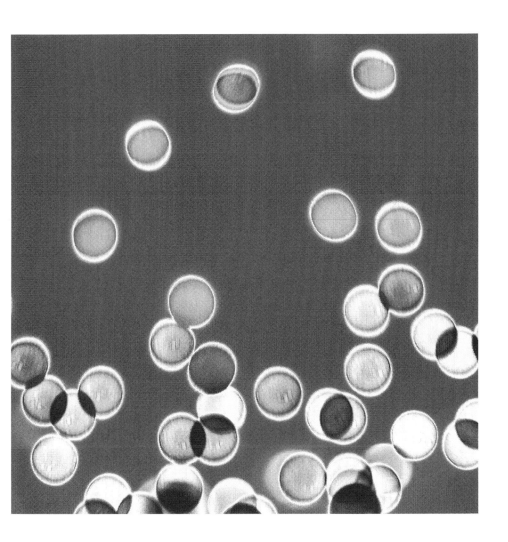

SKELETON

man is lonely
Dead behind alcohol washed eyes
Working hard.
His frail skeleton working harder
To hold up his tight leather cage
Bruised by age, worn
Scars deep, bar brawl rage.

He leans slowly and carefully
Brittle fingers, crept
Reaching down to his tobacco pouch
His back pocketed companion
His lone man routine.

Thin paper rolling maps,
Wrapped then slowly placed between
Pursed lips, for comfort
And peace
Looking out towards to the sky
In search for the opposite
His dreams slowly
Burnt into ash.

Breezed brushed

A single tear across

His wrinkled cheek

Reflecting out.

Feeling into the moons pale light

Illuminating a mirror image

The graveyard

.

## TRADITIONAL METHOD

伝統的な方法

Traditional Methods,
Just one, pays.


Poetry to pour the liquid thought
The clay cast, vessel, caught.
20 tons of sadness given unapologetically,
The smelting down of pandemonium.
Leaving only the extraction of raw emotion,
Not fully molten,
But enough to rest on the soft pine charcoal of devotion.


What now?
To be forged
Into interpretation,
A page flip
And peaceful resignation.

*Mr Peroxide*

A page flip

And peaceful resignation

## BETWEEN THE TROCADERO AND CHINATOWN

There are times, not often
Bored as a 50's housewife
There's two rolled
Flying through blood red eye
To hark back to my time with you.

Dusted book I pulled you out
The mental mausoleum
Brushed off the cobwebs
Surely not
Even fuller now
These memories damaged
Salvaged.

I can feel that London rain
Breeze between each building
Guided by your eye.
Your subtle
Eager hand to hold mine
Too nervous
I remember

Piccadilly was bright
Somehow, I always thought you shone brighter

I had tried to walk ahead
You called me back
Down a shielded cobbled alley
I never understood why you didn't like the rain.
Handing me one
We got high one last time
Between the Trocadero and Chinatown

CAFÉ


We sat, slid into a tanned leather booth
That was only to house us two
Lit harshly by autumnal sunlight
Reflecting off tiled walls
Home to photos of old Hollywood actors
That stood 6 inches taller than you.

We talked, tortured each other
Over complications that couldn't resolve to
Mugs stained by caffeinated dissolve.
Our eyes weary, distracted
As tangerine slid into
Evening, signalling
It was time we should be leaving.

I waited, waitress came but
You were preoccupied
Looking at your phone to even notice
Simple conclusions like nightfall
Or that the bill had been paid for,
Or that I had even left.

FOR FREE


Have you always taken so selfishly?

Learning lessons vicariously through me.

Like I am a New York $5

All you can eat buffet.

You may not go up for free

I am not merely there for

Mouthfuls upon mouthfuls.

So cheaply, you may not try before you buy

For I am fine wine to be tasted once then paid for.


My words to you are not free

Like they once were

It is for my friends.

You who seem to have shown their true colours

Charged double for the time that you take of mine

So selfishly, greedily.


My advice to you now

One last piece of me,

Would be to go

Go and live life

And then those lessons

You will learn for yourself, for free.

## HEALING NOW

Sunken eyes focused
Blinded by summer sun
Looking from the deep green of the foundations where you grow
Up to a sea of purple shades swaying softly in a summer breeze
Surrounded by the skies blue canvas
Nicely framed by the trees.

Walked through eagerly
But steadily
Not realising I had left you behind
Again.

I closed my eyes and took in the Lavenders sweet gentle scent
Calm
Letting natures herbs work into my mind
Relaxing my body
Fields of lilac to lie in
Calm, the day gone by.

I unclenched my jaw
Dropped my shoulders
My hand to meet yours
Someone new.

Sunsets golden now

Silhouetting the trees

Taking the purple slowly into the night

Leaving scents of serenity and peace

To help send us to sleep.

Healing now.

## HYDRANGEA

Your sweet smell

Oh man

You are man,

Reviving breath

Terraforming each cell of my being

Down to each sinew

Hydrangea to the sun

Leaning softly growing slowly

Covered and private
Secluded walkthroughs alone
Kiss in the churchyard

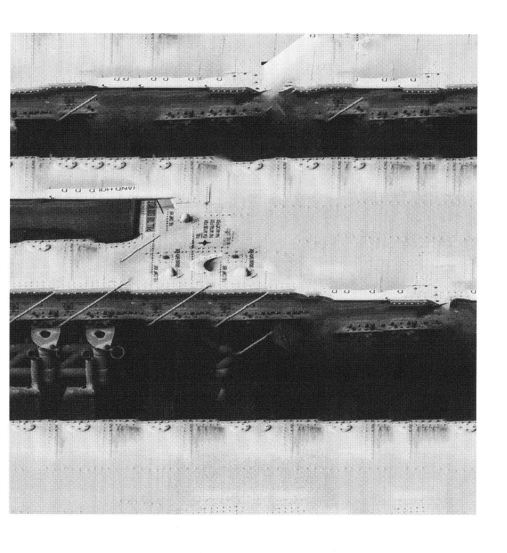

Discovery of the moons
Sat on the soft grass
Silvery quarter

Loving the night sky
Looking up to stars and strips
American Dream

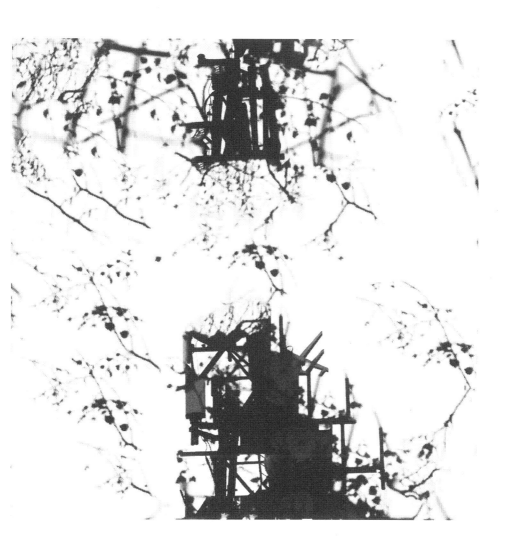

Slowly limbs moving
Lonely Yoga at midnight
Lavender to sleep

Petroleum air

Countryside living did bare

Fly me back to you

## UNFINISHED POEM TITLES

the train to London, or the train to nowhere?

stocks, shares and slings in Singapore

various museums, a world tour. Who for?

velvet grass

notifications off, hush the blue bird's song.

1947

the coffee shop next to the nightclub

Printer ink

A presidential election on my kitchen TV

Groom Lake Prince

WHY DOES LONDON NOT LOVE ME AS MUCH AS I LOVE IT

double jack

Staff Room Murder

# UNFINISHED POEM TITLES

thoughts on the set of a music video

23, a retrospective

Poker on the Space Station

6hrs of still

AMC to the Moon?

The Private Ear in the Public Eye

Tree

Houseplant

Panadol to Dexamyl

Fishbowl blues

Mr Z

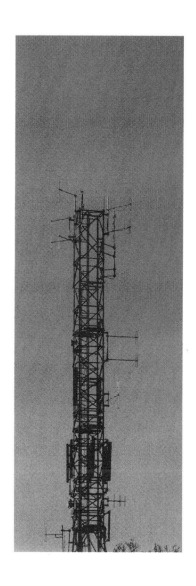

## NOTES AND ACKNOWLEDGMENTS

*'Sadness Given Unapologetically'* was written during the second lockdown of 2020. Thank you for being the first poem I wrote. This was the initial title for the book.

*'I Felt Sorry for Me'* is based at a London Club.

*'Traditional Method'* was based loosely on the forging of Japanese Swords.

*"Skeleton"* is read from the title

In the poem *'Healing Now'* I reference lavender fields, these are the lavender fields in Surrey.

If you haven't had the chance to read the poem *DESIDERATA* by Max Ehrmann, go and read it.

•

## NOTES AND ACKNOWLEDGMENTS

Thank you, to my biggest artistic influences: Marina Abramović, David Bowie, Lady Gaga, Matthew Healy, Sylvia Plath and Nina Simone

To my family for your continued support and love, thank you.

Thank you, Jess and Nathan for your constant encouragement and love during the creation of this project.

Thank you, to my English teacher Ms V. Ansa for educating me on art and life during my teen years.

# ABOUT THE AUTHOR

**Mr Peroxide** is a freelance LGBTQ+ photographer, artist and poet operating in Surrey and London. Having worked with companies for product photography and behind the scenes work for AVENUE, NO ROME and THE 1975

'Westerly Winds on Mars' is his first self-published book.

You can find his work with artists such as AVENUE, NO ROME and THE 1975 on his website or social media pages.

Instagram: Mr_Peroxide_

Website www.mrperoxidephotography.com

*Mr Peroxide*

*Mr Peroxide*

*A PLACE FOR POETRY AND PHOTOGRAPHY NOTES*

*A PLACE FOR POETRY AND PHOTOGRAPHY NOTES*

## *A PLACE FOR POETRY AND PHOTOGRAPHY NOTES*

*A PLACE FOR POETRY AND PHOTOGRAPHY NOTES*

*A PLACE FOR POETRY AND PHOTOGRAPHY NOTES*

*A PLACE FOR POETRY AND PHOTOGRAPHY NOTES*

*Mr Peroxide*

*A PLACE FOR POETRY AND PHOTOGRAPHY NOTES*

*A PLACE FOR POETRY AND PHOTOGRAPHY NOTES*

*A PLACE FOR POETRY AND PHOTOGRAPHY NOTES*

*A PLACE FOR POETRY AND PHOTOGRAPHY NOTES*

*A PLACE FOR POETRY AND PHOTOGRAPHY NOTES*

Printed in Great Britain
by Amazon